LET'S VISIT HONDURAS

Let's visit
HONDURAS

TRICIA HAYNES

First published 1985
© Tricia Haynes 1985

ACKNOWLEDGEMENTS

The Author and Publishers are grateful to the following organizations and individuals for permission to reproduce copyright photographs in this book:

Andes Press Agency; Anne Bolt; Susan Griggs Agency Limited; Instituto Hondureño de Turismo; The Mansell Collection Limited; Seaphot Limited; Photothèque Vautier-de Nanxe.

CIP data
Haynes, Tricia
  Let's visit Honduras
  1. Honduras – Social life and customs – Juvenile literature
  I. Title
  972.83'052   F1503.8
  ISBN 0 222 00959 4

Burke Publishing Company Limited
Pegasus House, 116-120 Golden Lane, London EC1Y 0TL, England.
Burke Publishing (Canada) Limited
Registered Office: 20 Queen Street West, Suite 3000, Box 30, Toronto, Canada M5H 1V5.
Burke Publishing Company Inc.
Registered Office: 333 State Street, PO Box 1740, Bridgeport, Connecticut 06601, U.S.A.
Filmset in Baskerville by Graphiti (Hull) Ltd., Hull, England.
Printed in Singapore by Tien Wah Press (Pte.) Ltd.

Contents

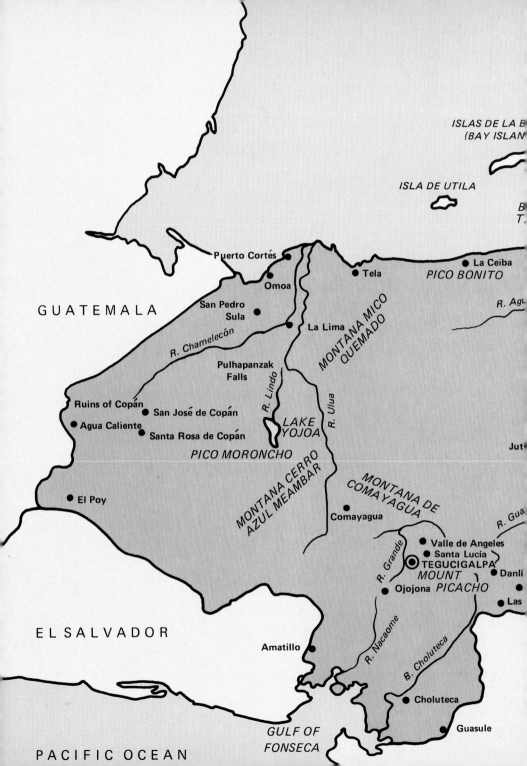

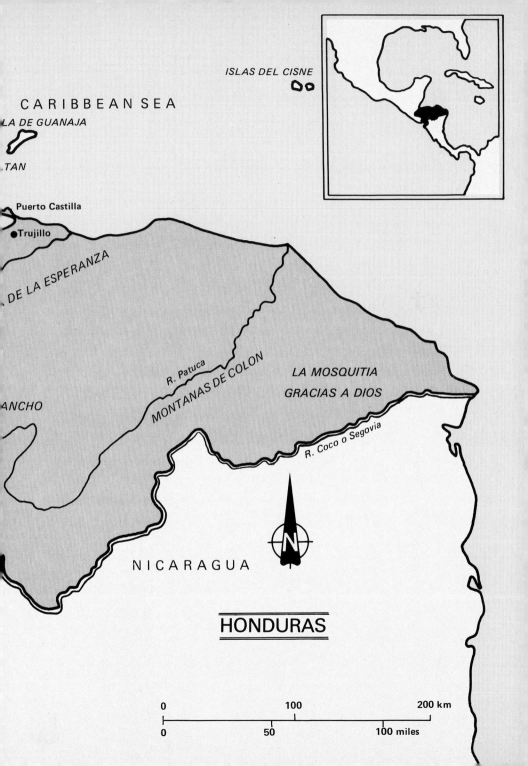

CARIBBEAN SEA

ISLAS DEL CISNE

LA DE GUANAJA

TAN

Puerto Castilla

Trujillo

DE LA ESPERANZA

R. Patuca

MONTAÑAS DE COLON

LA MOSQUITIA

GRACIAS A DIOS

ANCHO

R. Coco o Segovia

NICARAGUA

HONDURAS

0	100	200 km
0	50	100 miles

A Central American Republic

The Republic of Honduras, the second largest country in Central America, is shaped like a wedge, broader at one end than the other. It covers 114,000 square kilometres (44,000 square miles) and lies between Nicaragua, El Salvador and Guatemala. The border on the Guatemalan side stretches 340 kilometres (210 miles); the Nicaraguan border, 780 kilometres (490 miles), and the frontier with El Salvador, 340 kilometres (210 miles).

Honduras is bordered by the Pacific Ocean in the west, and the Caribbean Sea in the north. The Pacific coastline extends for 130 kilometres (80 miles), the Caribbean coastline for 645 kilometres (400 miles). Christopher Columbus gave to the country the name of Honduras, which in Spanish means "depth". A native of Honduras is called a *hondureño*.

Between 30 and 50 kilometres (20 to 30 miles) off Honduras' Caribbean shore lie the Bay Islands (Islas de la Bahia). The main islands in the group are Utila, Roatan and Guanaja. Closer to Nicaragua, about 96 kilometres (60 miles) from the coast, lie the tiny Islas del Cisne (Swan Islands). Both groups of islands belong to Honduras.

Honduras has many lakes and mountains. The main mountain ranges are the Cordillera Opalaca (running laterally

A village on the Caribbean coast. It was on the Bay Island of Guanaja off this coast that Christopher Columbus first landed

between El Salvador and Guatemala), Montaña de Comayagua, Sierra de la Esperanza, and Montañas de Colon. Flying in an aeroplane over the country reveals that more than eighty per cent of the land surface is covered by these ranges. The capital city of Tegucigalpa, for example, has so many mountains surrounding it that no jumbo jet could possibly land on its short airstrip.

Several peaks rise over 3,000 metres (about 10,000 feet). Pico Bonito, at whose foot lies the town of La Ceiba, is over 2,440 metres (8,000 feet). High valleys and plateaux separate the mountain areas, which are covered by forests of oak and pine.

9

The mountainous countryside around Tegucigalpa

For this reason Honduras has been given the name "Little Switzerland".

Honduras can be divided into four main areas: the Caribbean Lowlands known as La Costa, the coastal plains in the north-eastern part of the country called La Mosquitia, the Pacific Lowlands, and the highland mountain ranges with their dense rain forests, shrouded in thick, swirling mists. The rain forests begin at altitudes of 2,130 metres (about 7,000 feet). At such heights an abundance of huge trees, ferns, mosses and wild orchids grow. The orchid is the national flower of Honduras.

La Costa consists of river and coastal plains. The soil is so

10

fertile in the basin between the high ranges, that bananas and other tropical fruits grow well. Oranges, mandarins, lemons, pomelos (grapefruit), avocados and pineapples make money on the export markets. By comparison, La Mosquitia, the area that borders Nicaragua, is sparsely inhabited. Its resources have not yet been exploited, for visitors are rare there and the region barely explored.

Hunters have killed off much of Honduras' wildlife but, in remoter regions, tapirs, jaguars and ocelots can still be seen. Living in the forests are parrots, parakeets, macaws, humming-birds and birds of paradise. Wild ducks and bustards inhabit the swampier regions. In the lagoons there are many species of fish and in the coral reefs numerous sharks.

The Pacific Lowlands along the Gulf of Fonseca consist of savannah pastures—treeless plains covered with low vegetation—where Honduras' cattle is raised. Here the coastline

The orchid—the country's national flower

is only 145 kilometres (90 miles) long. These Lowlands produce sugar, cotton, tobacco, maize, coffee and bananas. Many species of brightly coloured butterflies are found in the savannah areas. As well as lofty mountain ranges, Honduras possesses valleys known as *valles*. These are covered by scrub and coarse grass, and form some of the country's most important cattle-raising areas.

Honduras has several major rivers which flow into the Pacific and Atlantic Oceans. The largest is the Ulua which is over 290 kilometres (180 miles) long. The Ulua and the Chamelecón bring water to the Sula plain making it extremely fertile. The Aguan river waters the Aguan valley which stretches almost 255 kilometres (158 miles), while the Patuca, 530 kilometres (330 miles) long, and its tributary, the Guayape, irrigate the plains of Olancho in the centre of Honduras. In places, the mighty Patuca river forms waterfalls as it flows across the country. But the longest river in Honduras is the Coco, also known as the Segovia. It flows for 800 kilometres (500 miles) along the frontier between Honduras and Nicaragua through the forests and swamps of the Mosquitia region. The two main rivers of the southern part of the country, both of which flow into the Pacific Ocean, are the Grande which flows through the capital Tegucigalpa, and the Nacaomé. Neither is as big, or as important, as the Coco river.

Although Honduras' lakes may not compare in size with those of neighbouring Nicaragua, Lake Yojoa—19 kilometres (12 miles) long, and 11 kilometres (7 miles) wide—is important due to its geographical position. It lies in the mountain region between Tegucigalpa and San Pedro Sula and forms a natural reservoir at an altitude of 640 metres (2,100 feet). Between the mountains and the Caribbean coast lie jungles, lakes, lagoons, and sandy beaches shaded by palms. Honduras is the only Central American republic which does not have volcanoes. And it has not suffered an earthquake for many centuries.

Honduras has a low population figure. There are about twenty-nine people per square kilometre (seventy-five per square mile), but because of the mountainous terrain—which in many areas cannot be cultivated—the population is not evenly spread. Two-thirds of the people live in the southern and western highlands. The other third live in towns and cities. In recent years, the growth of these urban areas has forced farmers to move into the Caribbean Lowlands to find new agricultural land.

Today the population stands at four million. Ninety-three per cent is *mestizo* (of mixed Spanish and American Indian origin), American Indian, or Caucasian (White). Blacks make up the rest. There is little trace of Indian culture left. The Paya, known as the Jungle People, inhabit the Mosquito Coast. The Miskito Indians live on the banks of the Coco river. Black Carib Indians live along the Caribbean coast. They are known as *morenos* or Garifunas, descendants of Carib Indians and Black slaves, brought from Africa to the West Indies and from there to Honduras. A colony of Caucasians inhabits the Bay Islands. Of these, only two per cent are pure-blooded whites. There are also some Chinese, who form their own settlements.

13

Like the vast majority of Honduras' population, this girl is a *mestizo*—of mixed Spanish and Indian origin

Although Honduras is situated in a tropical zone, its climate varies. The temperature on the coast may reach 25° Centigrade (77° Fahrenheit) while in the centre of the country it stays steady at 15 to 20° Centigrade (59 to 68° Fahrenheit). Rainfall is high, ranging from 500 to 760 millimetres (20 to 30 inches) in different regions. As a result of the rain, the country is green, with lush tropical vegetation.

14

Tegucigalpa, standing at an altitude of 915 metres (3,000 feet), enjoys a pleasant climate all year round, like many Highland towns. The daytime heat is tolerable due to the low humidity, and the evenings are always cool. The chilliest months are December and January. The dry season lasts from December to May. Rainy months in Highland areas are from June to September, while on the Atlantic coast, rainfall is at its heaviest from September to February. Coastal areas are hot, and get frequent rainfall throughout the year, although the rain lasts

A Black Carib boy, descended from Black slaves and Carib Indians

Tegucigalpa—the capital of Honduras—situated high in the mountains

for only a short period each day. In the Bay Islands and the Islas del Cisne ocean breezes temper the heat.

The official language of Honduras is Spanish. English is also spoken in the bigger towns and cities like Tegucigalpa and San Pedro Sula, and in the Bay Islands where many inhabitants are the descendants of British and French settlers. The Blacks speak a dialect known as Creole English.

Most Hondurans are Roman Catholic, but there are other religious denominations such as Anglican, Methodist, Baptist and Mormon.

16

The Honduran unit of currency is the *lempira*, which is divided into one hundred *centavos*, and comes in notes of one, five, ten, twenty and one hundred. The currency is named after the Indian chief and national hero, Lenca Lempira, who was killed in the sixteenth century while resisting Spanish attack. Two *lempira* equal one US dollar. *Centavos* come in coins of different values. A *búfalo* is the equivalent of the US nickel (five cents), a *toston* equals a quarter (twenty-five cents).

Hondurans have several public holidays. These are New Year's Day, Day of the Americas (April 14), International Labour Day (May 1), Independence Day (September 15), Columbus Day (October 12), and Army Day (October 21). On October 3 all Hondurans honour the birth of General Francisco Morazan who is a national hero. They also celebrate *fiestas* (festivals). One of the largest of these is the Feria San Isidro which takes place in the town of La Ceiba during the third week of May. The Feria Sampedrana is celebrated in San Pedro Sula in June. Dancing in the streets, bicycle races and all kinds of celebrations feature in these festivals, and every Honduran joins in the fun.

These days visitors to the country usually arrive by air, landing at Toncontin airport, 5 kilometres (3 miles) from Tegucigalpa. The flight takes six hours from New York, and fifteen from London. San Pedro Sula also has an airport, named Dr. Ramon Villeda Morales, after one of the republic's presidents. So does the town of La Ceiba, making three international airports in all.

The border between Honduras and El Salvador. It is sometimes closed because of disputes

The French Line and the Royal Netherland Steamship Company operate shipping lines to Honduras, and offer a limited passenger service. It is possible to drive from Guatemala and Nicaragua, though relations between El Salvador and Honduras are not always good and the route between those two countries is sometimes closed. Once in Honduras, it is easy to get around by car or bus. Traffic travels on the right, as it does in all Central and South American countries. Local bus services connect the main towns, while Tica International Service buses go out of the country to all the Central American capitals.

18

The Honduran flag is easy to recognize. It is blue and white with a cluster of five-pointed blue stars. Like most countries, Honduras has its own special customs, and if you want to feel at home, it is a good idea to note them. Hondurans appreciate politeness. They themselves are friendly and easy-going. They treat foreigners respectfully and welcome them to their country.

As the Honduran nation is composed of various races, let us find out how so many different peoples came to live together.

Independence from Spain

From the third to the tenth century, a race known as the Maya inhabited the land. They cultivated maize, using it not only as a staple food, but also as an object of worship. They considered it to be their god. Soon they developed their own culture and their civilization flourished, until the capital city of Copán collapsed in the tenth century and the Maya disappeared.

Between the eleventh and sixteenth centuries, Honduras was almost forgotten. Native inhabitants, known as Amerindians, were living in the territory, but no one knew whether their ancestors had come from South-East Asia by way of the Pacific, or directly from Asia by way of the land mass which, at that time, filled the gap between the north-east corner of Asia and the north-west corner of North America.

When Christopher Columbus set foot in Honduras in 1502, on his fourth and last voyage to the New World, he saw only traces of the Maya culture. He arrived in July on the Island of Guanaja (one of the Bay Islands) and, seeing that the land was covered in pine trees, called it the Island of Pines.

Honduras is often buffeted by high winds and, after leaving the island, Columbus' ships were obliged to seek shelter. His brother, Bartolomé, landed in the Bay of Trujillo on the Caribbean coast and claimed Honduras in the name of the king of Spain.

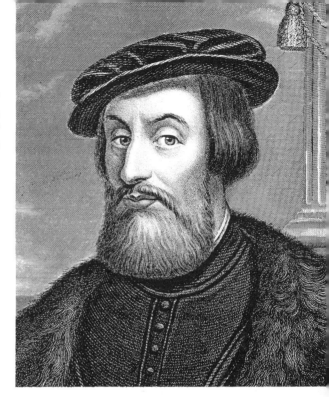

The Spanish explorer Hernán Cortés who founded the city of Puerto Cortés

After Columbus came many Spanish conquistadors (conquerors) whose chief objective was to find gold and silver. The explorer Hernán Cortés was among them. Arriving from Mexico, he founded the city of Puerto Cortés. From Panama, in 1524, came Gil Gonzales de Avila who had it in mind to colonize the territory, but Hernán Cortés managed to outwit him. Cortés sent Cristobal de Olid with an army of Spaniards to capture the land for him. Olid carried out his orders and took possession of Honduras, but instead of bequeathing it to Cortés he kept it for himself. A furious Cortés, who had returned to Mexico, was obliged to march to Honduras to win back the land which Olid had conquered in his name. However, when he

21

arrived, he discovered that Cristobal de Olid had already been executed on a charge of treason.

Meanwhile, Pedrarias the Cruel, governor of Panama, also had his eye on Honduras and battles broke out between the settlers and his forces. Eventually, Pedrarias was defeated and the settlers took the land. During this period the conquistadors were fighting the native Indian tribes for their gold and silver. They planned to make the Indians work in the mines and then hand the gold and silver over to them. The Indians who refused were promptly killed by the conquistadors, and Black slaves were brought from the West Indies and Africa to help the Spaniards in their search for gold. Very soon black and white people intermarried, and a colony began to emerge with mixed races as its inhabitants. But not before terrible slaughter had taken place.

Lenca Lempira, chief of an Indian tribe, and his army of thirty thousand men, managed to resist the Spanish attack. Hernán Cortés had sent Pedro de Alvarado to Honduras to end the rebellion, but Lempira was ready for him. However, he did make the mistake of believing Alvarado when he promised a truce. Lempira left his fortress and was killed by the conquistadors. He became Honduras' national hero. His name was given to the unit of currency, and stands as a symbol of liberty.

However, it was not only by land that armies arrived. Navigators came from the sea, round Cape Horn, and began exploring the Pacific coast. Like the conquistadors who came as mercenaries and adventurers, they had heard of the fabulous gold and silver mines. Tegucigalpa, whose Indian name means "Silver Hill", was found to be particularly rich in the metals, and many speculators journeyed to scoop up its treasures.

On his explorations of the Pacific coast during the sixteenth century, Gil Gonzales de Avila discovered the Gulf of Fonseca. He was followed in the seventeenth and eighteenth centuries by bands of buccaneers and pirates who swarmed up and down the Central American coast. They hid themselves on the islands where they could best observe the Spanish galleons journeying back to Spain with their treasures.

The Bay Islands were the pirates' most accessible hiding-places, and they operated with great good fortune. The Island of Roatan, with its ideal outlet, French Harbour, was the pirate Henry Morgan's base, while French and Dutch buccaneers

The Island of Roatan where the pirate Henry Morgan established his base

The seventeenth-century pirate Henry Morgan, notorious for his attacks on Spanish galleons, as they sailed home with their cargo of gold and silver

roamed the coasts, looting and pillaging. Today, Honduran archives record the stories of many such pirates who patrolled the seas until British forces commanded the Mosquito Coast and Bay Islands, and maintained them until 1859. A treaty was then drawn up, which returned the land to Honduras.

By the turn of the nineteenth century, the people of Honduras were growing restless. They declared they wanted independence from Spain and, in 1821, for a short period, Honduras was able to break free. Its population was no more than 200,000, and

24

in 1823 it became part of the United Provinces of Central America. The president of the Union of Central American Provinces was Francisco Morazan, who was born in Tegucigalpa and was a great believer in uniting Central America. Valiantly he tried to keep the provinces together, but from the start he was beset by economic and social difficulties. At last, in 1838, Honduras became an independent republic, but many Hondurans still wanted a unified Central America.

Francisco Morazan continued to work for unity. He was called the "Defender of Central America" and, after his death in 1842, was declared a national hero. Monuments, parks and statues were laid out to commemorate him. After Morazan's death, there followed a century of unrest. Riots, rebellions and wars with other Central American countries were the order of the day. Politically, Honduras was in a mess. Conservatives battled with Liberals, resulting in Honduras earning the reputation of being one of the most unstable countries in Central America.

Finally, in 1957, Dr. Ramon Villeda Morales, a member of the Liberal Party, was elected president. Roads were built. A social security system was begun. But progress was soon disrupted when, in 1963, a military coup headed by General Osvaldo Lopez Arellano, drove Morales from office. The military *junta* (council), headed by Arellano, maintained limited parliamentary power until 1972, when it took full control of the country. But in 1975 Arellano was dismissed from office, accused of accepting a million-dollar bribe from the United Fruit Company. Once again, Honduras found itself in difficulties.

How Honduras Functions

The military regime continued for the next few years until, in 1981, a civilian government was established. In Honduras, political elections are held every four years when a president and National Congress are appointed. The present head of state is President Roberto Suazo Cordova, who was elected when the Liberal Party came to power in 1981 with a fifty-three per cent majority.

The Liberal Party, and its opposite number, the National Party, are the two largest political factions. Two smaller parties, Partido Demócrata Cristiano which has one seat, and Partido

The changing of the guard at the Presidential Palace in Tegucigalpa

An armed guard for an important arrival at Toncontin Airport, outside Tegucigalpa

Innovación y Unidad, with three seats, are also represented in Congress. There are 1.5 million registered voters, of which eighty-two per cent voted in the 1981 election.

Honduras has an army composed of fifteen thousand men which includes a five hundred strong police force. Officers are generally well disciplined, spending part of their training period abroad. At present the number of officers is about two thousand. The rest of the army consists of the poor people who aim to work their way up through the ranks to become officers. As Honduras is one of the poorest countries in Central America, many young men join the army instead of looking for work elsewhere.

Because the standard of living is generally low, the

27

import/export market is small. Honduras has been seriously affected by the fluctuation of coffee prices in recent years just when its coffee production is rising, and by import costs which have greatly increased. Since most Honduran industry is based on products like coffee, bananas, sugar and lumber, the country is limited as far as improving its output is concerned, though efforts are being made to extend its coffee and banana plantations and to grow new crops like cocoa and spices. The timber industry is doing well. Forests are one of the country's best resources, producing high quality mahogany, pine, oak, teak and balsa.

During the last ten years, Hondurans have had to endure several disasters. In 1974, Hurricane Fifi caused widespread damage and serious flooding, as well as many deaths. It was followed by a drought in 1975. The country has also suffered from the increase in oil prices—and from the fact that its political system has not always been stable, with border disputes often erupting between Honduras and neighbouring El Salvador.

After the 1974 hurricane disaster, Honduras was forced to seek help from other countries in order to get the economy back on its feet. In 1980, the United Kingdom made a five million pound loan for the development of agriculture and the provision of other necessities. Part of the money was used for hospital equipment, coffee sprayers, and installations to improve water supplies. Monetary help has also been received to improve the fisheries and the forestry areas. In 1982 the United States' economic aid to Honduras amounted to almost three million

These men are harvesting sugar-cane—one of Honduras' most important crops

US dollars for technical help, and over fourteen million US dollars in financial aid.

Despite this financial assistance however, it will take several years to put the trade balance right. Meanwhile Honduras is doing its best to develop those industries which can earn money for the country. Coffee has now reached an output of seventeen per cent, bananas forty-three per cent and timber fifteen per cent of the country's total exports. Timber exports bring in forty-five million US dollars annually.

Honduras' economy is boosted by its mineral resources which include gold, silver, lead, iron, copper, tin, zinc and mercury. Traces of oil and iron deposits have been discovered, while semiprecious stones like onyx, agate, opals and jade can also be found. The republic's main customer for lead and zinc is Western Europe. Its chief suppliers of industrial products like chemicals, fertilizers and transport equipment are the United States and Britain.

Maize and beans are Honduras' main staple crops and these comprise the staple diet of many of its people. Rice, cotton, tobacco, and tropical fruits such as pineapples, melons and grapefruit are also plentiful in the country. Wheat is imported from the United States.

Agriculture is the basis of the national economy, although less than a quarter of the total land area is cultivated. Of this quarter, woodland and forest account for more than sixty-one per cent, pasture land for twenty-five per cent, and arable

Outside Tegucigalpa—the timber industry's high-quality exports are an important source of income for the country

Picking grapefruit—they are so heavy that it is easier to throw them to someone down below than to put them into baskets

land for ten per cent. Banana-growing is concentrated on the Lowlands of the northern part of the country. La Mosquitia is not cultivated, but many mountain areas are being considered as regions suitable for the development and expansion of agriculture. As so much of the territory is under-populated, stock-raising has been developed as a source of income. Today, Honduras can count over 1,500,000 head of cattle, and 500,000

31

pigs, and meat is becoming an important export. The cattle, a cross of European and Central American breeds, are reared to withstand the tropical climate. Poultry is plentiful.

Since there are very few good roads, much of the travelling across the savannahs is still by mule or donkey. In agricultural areas this is the normal form of transportation; mule carts and men on horseback are a very familiar sight. Modern means of communication have not yet reached many parts of the agricultural communities.

The fishing industry is also backward. While Honduras has eight ports, and the republic's territorial waters extend 320 kilometres (200 miles) off the coast, lack of supervision and control result in fishermen from other countries poaching in Honduran waters. In the Gulf of Fonseca on the Pacific, and off much of the Caribbean coastline, there are many species of fish; but while catches are substantial, fisheries are small and no large-scale preservation facilities yet exist. Shellfish are important to Honduras, accounting for sixty per cent of the fishing catch. Prawns and crayfish are exported to the United States. Lagoons, like Lake Yojoa, have plentiful supplies of fresh-water fish, such as bass which is sold in the local markets. However, until the fisheries develop on a larger scale, much of the fish cannot be properly used.

With the help of foreign aid, industry is now making progress. Manufacturing industries such as cotton spinning, weaving, cigarette manufacture, dairy and fruit production and meat

Loading bananas in the port of Tela for shipment to the United States and Europe

freezing and packing are beginning to make headway.

Like Panama, Honduras operates a ''flag of convenience'', which means that ships flying the Honduran flag have paid a fee to register their boats in Honduras, although they may come from any part of the world. Puerto Cortés, one of the country's major ports, operated by the National Port Undertaking, has a Free Zone (in which imported goods are not subject to tax). With its deep-water harbour it is one of the best equipped ports on the Atlantic coast. Also on Honduras' Atlantic seaboard are the ports of Tela and La Ceiba. Tela is used mainly for the

33

shipment of bananas, but La Ceiba actually exports more bananas and pineapples than any other port in Honduras. Farther east lies the port of Trujillo/Castilla; and, in the Bay Islands, the port of Roatan.

All imported goods not in a Free Zone are subject to a duty, calculated on the gross weight of the merchandise. In 1981 an additional duty was added on all imports except medical supplies and powdered milk. All imported goods over $5,000 in value must have authorization from the Banco Central de Honduras, the country's national bank.

Though Honduras is a poor country, and is so far under-developed, with the aid of foreign money it is beginning to move towards a better economic future.

Living in Honduras

The mountainous terrain of the country means that communities in Honduras are often isolated. Many of the remote *pueblos* (villages) are more than four hundred years old. Their adobe houses (made of dried earth) have red tiled roofs. These communities often have white, colonial-style churches, cobbled streets and a town square where the *pueblo*-dwellers like to gather to exchange news. Some are old mining towns which, in the sixteenth century, supplied gold and silver to the Spaniards. These days many of the mines no longer operate, and the

Houses built in colonial style

In the poorer city areas
of Honduras there are
many wooden houses
like this one, built on
stilts

inhabitants of the towns have turned to agriculture for their livelihood. Small farms bring in a fairly regular source of income.

In mountain communities, traditional crafts are still practised. The inhabitants often sit outside their homes, making baskets, embroidering and sewing—producing the typical handicrafts visitors buy in cities like Tegucigalpa and San Pedro Sula at much higher prices.

In the port cities of Puerto Cortés, La Ceiba and Tela, narrow streets lead down to the harbour. In the downtown sectors and the dock areas, the houses are often shabby. Tela is a lively town, with some of the best beaches in Honduras, while La Ceiba has an easy-going atmosphere.

In the old part of La Lima, known as Lima Vieja, there are rows of small houses made of clapboard or corrugated iron where the workers of the banana plantations live. In contrast, the managers live in large homes surrounded by lush, tropical gardens. In San Pedro Sula there are many fine homes in the residential district of Bella Vista, while in Tegucigalpa, and in the old colonial town of Jutiapa, some colonial-style houses still remain.

On the Bay Islands, the Black Carib Indians have built quaint villages near the water, which they like better than the isolated farmsteads lived in by the mainlanders.

Honduras has two airlines flying international routes. These are SAHSA (Servicio Aereo de Honduras SA) and TAN (Transportes Aereos Nacionales). SAHSA connects Honduras to other Central American countries. TAN flies to Belize, Miami (USA) and Mexico City, as well as to domestic destinations like San Pedro Sula and La Ceiba.

Once the American fruit companies moved into the banana plantations they soon obtained concessions to extend the railway. The narrow gauge railroad lines were constructed principally for the use of the plantations as they extended along the northern coast. These lines stretch for 822 kilometres (511 miles), while the national system runs for only 245 kilometres (152 miles), between Puerto Cortés and San Pedro Sula. There are limited passenger services, and trains do not have restaurant cars.

The best way to get around in Honduras is by road. There are 8,000 kilometres (5,000 miles) of roads, but only about twenty per cent of them are paved. These asphalted roads have been built over the past twenty-five years, and their condition is still reasonably good. Other roads are little more than uneven surface tracks. The Inter-American Highway runs from Amatillo on the border with El Salvador in the west, through the southern

Maize is part of the staple diet in Honduras. This woman will sell what she cooks to passers-by

part of the country to Guasule on the border with Nicaragua. This route covers a distance of 153 kilometres (95 miles).

From Tegucigalpa, the Oriental Highway travels for 148 kilometres (92 miles) through Danlí and El Paraíso, ending at Las Manos on the border with Nicaragua. From north to south, a trunk road connects the Atlantic with the Pacific coasts, passing through La Ceiba and Tela.

The Western Highway runs for about 300 kilometres (210 miles) from San Pedro Sula to Agua Caliente on the border with Guatemala, and to El Poy on the border with El Salvador. The remainder of the country must rely on 3,380 kilometres (2,100 miles) of roads, and some communities are completely isolated. In La Mosquitia, the population has clustered on the coast, making this one of the most undeveloped areas of the country.

In spite of its lack of suitable roads for vehicles, there is a bus service from the two main cities of Tegucigalpa and San Pedro Sula to various parts of the country. Regular buses leave Tegucigalpa for Choluteca, Danlí and El Paraíso and from San Pedro Sula to Puerto Cortés, Tela and La Ceiba. The buses leave from the main squares of Tegucigalpa and San Pedro Sula, and travel through the suburbs and villages. They are crowded and noisy, with all kinds of people taking rides because fares are cheap. Buses are generally as fast as taxis and cost a great deal less. Those who do travel by taxi will notice that Honduran taxicabs have no meters, so it is best to ask the cost before getting in (people are not expected to tip the driver unless they want to!). Taxis may be hired by the hour by those who

39

Crowded buses in San Pedro Sula—bus travel is cheap, and noisy!

want to spend time looking around. Hondurans do not always rely on public transport. They also like to drive, and at present there are between 80,000 and 100,000 vehicles in the republic.

As more people travel to Honduras, there is a need for more hotels to be built. Three new ones have recently opened in Tegucigalpa and more have been constructed in La Ceiba and on the Bay Islands. A resort country club has opened at Lake Yojoa, and in 1982 a first-class tourist hotel opened in Santa Rosa de Copán.

Restaurants of international class usually serve American dishes, but smaller, more modest establishments offer local specialities like *mondongo* (a type of soup), *frijoles* (beans), *tapado* (stew), mangoes, papaya and avocados. For many families, everyday Honduran food consists of *tortillas* (omelettes) or *plato típico* (fried egg, meat, beans and plantains). Like their Central American neighbours, Hondurans make much use of bananas in their cooking, and also of maize, a necessary ingredient in such dishes as *tamales* (corn pancakes).

Public health conditions are generally good, and malaria has almost disappeared. Nevertheless, it is not safe to drink water from taps—better to use bottled or purified water. Honduras has one doctor for every two thousand people, and seven public hospitals in its bigger cities. Several private hospitals exist in Tegucigalpa and San Pedro Sula.

Gradually educational standards are improving and the literacy rate is now about forty-two per cent. Primary education is free, and compulsory. More teachers are being recruited. The University of Tegucigalpa and its extension Ciudad Universitaria (University City), provide about twenty thousand students with low-cost higher education.

The birth-rate is high, but many women see no reason to enter into marriage as the country provides health and medical care for their offspring.

Government and business hours are from 8.00 am to 5.00 pm. Banking hours are from 8.30 am to 12.00 noon and from 2.00 pm to 3.00 pm. There are several banks in Honduras, including the Banco Central de Honduras. As the national bank, it controls the exchange of currency—usually only US dollars

and travellers cheques in US dollars can be exchanged.

Telecommunications are getting better. There were 27,000 telephones in 1980, and the figure grows each year. International calls can be made from Honduras to the United Kingdom, the United States, and other major countries. Telegrams and telexes can be sent from the offices of the Tropical Radio Company in Tegucigalpa and San Pedro Sula.

The republic has three television services: Channels 3 and 5 in Tegucigalpa, and Channels 3 and 7 in San Pedro Sula.

Radio Honduras is the official government station. Other radio stations are commercially run.

For those who like to keep up with the news, Honduras has five main newspapers. In Tegucigalpa, there are *El Día, La Tribuna,* and *El Cronista*; in San Pedro Sula, *La Prensa* and *El Tiempo.* Although there are no English-language newspapers in Honduras, the *Miami Herald* is usually available in hotel lobbies.

Main towns have theatres and cinemas which show American films as well as Spanish-language ones. When they are shopping, most visitors look for Honduran cigars, woodcarvings, ceramics, black coral, jade, string hammocks (you can see many of these in the beach areas), articles of straw and macramé (knotted thread). Local artists have begun to do brisk business with their paintings, many of which find their way to the galleries of the United States or to other parts of the world.

Futbol (soccer) is the national sport. The game is played at the National Stadium in Tegucigalpa, and in the Morazan Municipal Stadium in San Pedro Sula. Other towns and villages have their own football fields. Though Honduran footballers often play without shoes, the game is taken seriously, and on Thursdays and Sundays when the main cities stage their League games, crowds of people can be seen making for the soccer pitches.

Baseball is almost as popular, especially in the Bay Islands. Golf and tennis figure lower on the list, but hiking and climbing are favourite pastimes. Honduras has plenty of mountains to climb, mist-shrouded rain forests and remote villages to explore.

Water sports come high on the list of priorities. Some of the best snorkelling is off the Bay Islands. Strings of coral reefs are just waiting to be explored. But permission is needed to dive down to investigate the wrecks of Spanish galleons on the seabed. Spanish treasures still lie there, untouched for centuries.

Hondurans can find a variety of things to do in their leisure time, but how do they go about earning a living?

Earning a Living

With almost seventy-five per cent of the workforce employed in agriculture, and only twelve per cent in industry, the Honduran government is keen to extend its agriculture programme so that its products can earn more in the world's export markets. In this respect Honduras is fortunate, for its banana plantations provide a steady source of income. Indeed, Honduras, along with other Central American countries, has been dubbed a "banana republic".

La Lima is one of the fastest-growing cities in Latin America—since 1950 it has expanded almost one thousand per cent. This banana company town, constructed by the United Fruit Company, contains offices, a research laboratory and houses for its employees. There are also two schools, so children can be educated right in the plantations. Many *trabajadores* (workers) are employed in this vast, industrial plant, where they select, pack and stack bananas onto trains bound for the docks. There the fruit is loaded onto ships and taken right across the world.

Bananas which are slightly damaged, or those not up to export standard, are used in baby foods, and for flavouring ice-cream, cakes and pastries. They are processed at plants usually separated from the main complex, called *bananinas* (little

Bananas from the United Fruit Company being loaded for transportation by rail to the ports of Tela and Puerto Cortés

bananas), for the bananas rejected for export are often too small to conform to standard sizes and to exacting quality controls.

For more than seventy-five years, bananas were the richest source of income for the republic. However, in 1974 there was a major disaster when Hurricane Fifi destroyed nearly all the banana crop. Since then, Honduras has attempted to improve its production, although bananas have now been overtaken by coffee as the republic's major export. Honduran coffee, like its tobacco, sells well in the world's markets. Since 1977 production has increased, which means the industry can employ more of the country's workforce.

It was bananas, however, that enabled Honduras to be a contender in the highly competitive export market and helped improve its trade figures. During the nineteenth century, when the north-east consisted mainly of Lowland jungles, North American companies were offered concessions by the Honduran government, to develop the land. The people of the highland areas had no desire to move to work in the hot, humid coastal plains, which were rife with disease, so the American companies hired their own labour. There was plenty of work to be done before banana production could go into full operation. Railroads

Bananas like these, which are not up to standard, are made into purée and used in baby-foods, ice-cream, cakes and pastries

needed to be built, and installations constructed at ports like Puerto Cortés and La Ceiba. And so, West Indian workers were brought in.

Once the industry got started, this fact caused dissatisfaction among the local inhabitants. They now thought they should be employed rather than the West Indians who had been brought in over their heads. They had to be content, however, with the fact that by then the banana industry was making a great deal of money for the country. Nevertheless, disputes often broke out between the various races, and even today there is a big division between the people of the Highlands and those of the Lowland areas.

On the outskirts of San Pedro Sula there is another plantation, and a packing plant called Finca San Juan. If you walk through a banana plantation you will see that the huge clusters of bananas grow with their tips pointing upwards and not down. When the big purple banana flower falls off, you can see the fruits which start off as tiny green bananas and gradually expand and ripen. The bunches of bananas are then covered by plastic bags to keep *in* the humidity and keep *out* insects which would destroy them. If they were not protected in this way, the fierce sun would scorch them and the crop would be wasted.

Once the bananas have ripened sufficiently, each bunch is marked by a coloured string indicating when it should be cut. One week it may be the bunches marked by a red string, the following, the bunches tied with a blue tag, so that the bananas are cut in rotation, and only when they are absolutely ready.

48

They cannot be allowed to grow too ripe, for they must be packed while they are still green, and before they turn yellow.

When the bunches are cut, they are hooked onto an overhead cable system, and this "train" of bananas is then conveyed into the packing shed. The workers cut the bananas into "hands" which are much smaller bunches. They are then washed and packed. Finally they are stacked onto trains and taken to Puerto Cortés where they are loaded aboard cargo ships sailing for the United States and Europe.

Puerto Cortés, which handles the bananas of the United Fruit Company, has a population of around 50,000 and is one of the most modern ports in Central America. As well as bananas, other tropical fruits grown in the Sula Valley are handled here. In fact this busy port copes with over half the imports and exports of Honduras. Its Free Zone enables it to be used for the wholesale export of goods, and its oil refinery is now one of the best in Central America. Buses leave every thirty minutes from the port to San Pedro Sula, so workers can commute each day.

Tela, with a population of 20,000 is also used chiefly for the export of bananas. Before moving to La Lima, the United Fruit Company had its headquarters here and these have now been transformed into a resort complex with shops selling all kinds of souvenirs.

In 1926 the United Fruit Company was responsible for laying out the extensive Botanical Gardens in Tela. At this time, the Company was afraid that disease might wipe out the banana plantations and, in order to discover the kind of plants best suited as replacements, cultivated many different species. However, the plantations survived, and today it is the citizens of Tela and visitors to the town who can enjoy the Botanical Gardens, and observe the many kinds of birds who make their home there.

Over the last few years, a number of small-scale industries have sprung up in San Pedro Sula, Honduras' second largest town and chief commercial centre. The sugar industry and the

The plantation at La Lima. Plastic bags are used to protect the bananas until they are ripe enough to harvest

Surprisingly perhaps, as shown here, bananas are washed before they are packed

furniture industry are improving. There is also production of plywood, matches, plastic goods, paper goods, cigars, cigarettes, oils and fats such as lard and coconut oil.

Don Pedro de Alvarado founded San Pedro Sula in 1536. Over the following four hundred years it remained an agricultural town. The land was particularly fertile, and crops grew fast, so labourers could be occupied for much of the year. After the Second World War, San Pedro Sula's industry began to develop, and very soon the town was being hailed as the industrial capital of the republic. The population has increased ten times in the last thirty years, and now stands at 200,000. Today, San Pedro Sula is a modern, busy place, with many

51

Palm fruits, also cultivated by the United Fruit Company

hotels, banks and office buildings. Employment opportunities have grown too, and many Hondurans have found work in this industrial city.

Situated 76 metres (250 feet) above sea level, the climate is hot and sticky, but *sanpedranos* (people from San Pedro Sula) are used to humid temperatures and scarcely notice the heat. The town lies in the most fertile agricultural zone of the republic and today is not only the commercial hub but also the main distribution centre of the region. It is an informal city, and its annual Fair, the Semana Sanpedrana (St. Peter's Week), which is held in June, includes handicraft stalls, exhibitions, flower displays and a big cattle show which is so popular it is necessary to make advance reservations.

Today little of the old city of San Pedro Sula remains. Most of it is modern, even the cathedral (Catedral de San Pedro Sula) which is still under construction. Although the facade looks colonial, it was begun after the Second World War in 1949.

As in most Central and South American cities, the streets are divided into *avenidas* (avenues) and *calles* (streets). Steep, winding roads take you past some of the most prosperous houses of the town—owned by managers and directors of industrial corporations—to the lookout of Mirador Capri. From here there is a fine view over the productive Sula Valley (once known as Valle de Choloma from the Indian word meaning Valley of Birds), to the mountains of El Tiburon, Mico Quemado,

Children working in a chalk quarry near San Pedro Sula

Meambar, and Pico Moroncho (Honduras' highest mountain).

In addition to its profitable manufacturing industries such as tobacco—Honduran cigars are considered to be of excellent quality—the country still relies on gold and silver. More people are employed in mineral resources than ever before.

With San Pedro Sula expanding so fast, how does this affect the Highland dweller whose mountain capital—Tegucigalpa—has managed to maintain much of its past traditions?

Tegucigalpa—The Mountain Capital

Tegucigalpa became the capital of Honduras in 1880. Long before that the Spanish invaders forced the Indians to work in the mines of Tegucigalpa to produce gold and silver to send back to Spain. By 1578 the mining industry had become so important that the Guatemalan authorities made Tegucigalpa the headquarters of the mining industry. (Honduras was not yet a republic and was ruled by a Captaincy-General in Guatemala). They called the city Real de Minas (Royal Mines) and it became the administrative centre for mining.

Situated at 915 metres (3,000 feet) on the slopes of Mount Picacho, Tegucigalpa has never suffered an earthquake, so much of its colonial history is still apparent. This high-altitude capital has a population of 500,000 and, due to its position, the temperature stays steady at about 24° Centigrade (75° Fahrenheit).

Tegucigalpa is a modern city with plenty of hotels and restaurants. Its shops sell all kinds of local handicrafts such as bead necklaces, leather-work, dried flowers, pottery and embroidery. The city stands on the banks on the Choluteca river and has not been laid out to order like some other capital cities. Streets run this way and that to dodge the surrounding hills. The influence of the Spaniards can be seen in some of the

The Honduran capital Tegucigalpa—its architecture is a mixture of colonial and modern styles

eighteenth- and nineteenth-century homes with their roofs made of round tiles, and their inner courtyards filled with shrubs and flowers. A view across the city shows rows of red roofs, different coloured houses and white colonial churches.

In common with all Central American cities, Tegucigalpa has a main square. It is called Plaza Morazan, and is named after Francisco Morazan who fought so hard for Central American unity. He is commemorated by an equestrian statue, around which the citizens of the town often place bunches of flowers. The busy square now forms part of the Parque Central (Central

Park). Here the people of the city walk, read or sit on benches by the fountain. Shoeshine boys (*limpias botas*) do good business in the park. One of the adjacent roads has recently been paved and closed to traffic, and La Peatonal, a pedestrian precinct planted with trees, has made this area a good meeting spot. No one has to worry about traffic any more—people can walk freely, or just sit in the sunshine.

Streets and avenues are mostly numbered. Only a handful of streets in Tegucigalpa have proper names like the Boulevard Morazan, Avenida Republica de Chile, Avenida La Paz, Avenida Juan Ramon Molina, and Avenida Puente 12 de Julio. The rest fall into *calles* and *avenidas*, but an A is usually added—calle 1A, 2A, avenida 6A and so on.

The bridges (*puentes*) crossing the city *do* have names. These are called Puente Goberania Nacional, Puente Maillol and

Modern bungalows in the new quarter of Tegucigalpa

Puente la Isla. The Casa Presidencial (Presidential Palace) is situated between the Goberania Nacional and Maillol bridges. The Puente Maillol, begun in 1818 and completed ten years later, is the oldest bridge in Tegucigalpa. On the banks of the river the Palace, built in 1919, looks like a fortress with its ramparts and watchtowers. Beside it, the Central Prison also has a forbidding look with its towers and parapets, but it is now a craft centre.

Close to Central Park is El Palacio Nacional (the National Palace), once the convent of San Sebastian. Later it became a hospital and, after that, the Edificio de los Ministerios (government offices.) Across the street where the Post Office (Correo Nacional) now stands, Honduras' first orphanage was founded. This later became its first medical school. On Avenida 6 at Calle 5, stands the house where General Francisco Morazan

The Plaza Morazan in Tegucigalpa

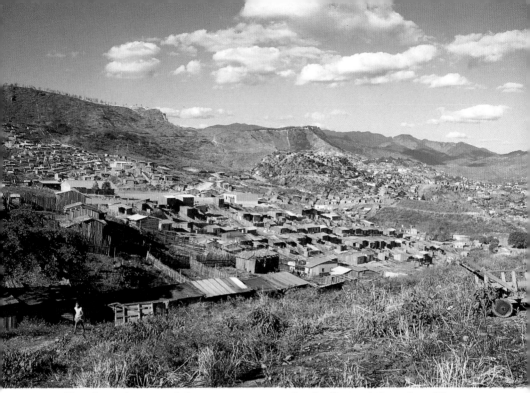

Honduras is one of the poorest countries in Central America. Many people live in shanty towns like this one in Tegucigalpa

was born in 1782. Today it is the National Library, and possesses thousands of books including history and geography books about Honduras.

Tegucigalpa has many colonial churches. The Catedral de San Miguel (St Michael), known as the Cathedral of Tegucigalpa, was built between 1756 and 1782 by Gregorio Quiroz. Indians made the font from a single block of stone in 1643, long before the cathedral was constructed. The silver altar was made by Vincente Galez.

The Church of the Virgin of Sorrows was built in 1732. Of

59

The Cathedral of Tegucigalpa

all the city's churches this one best illustrates the colonial style. Its brightly painted statues are excellent examples of local craftsmanship and its gold altar dates from 1742.

Close to the Parque Central is the late seventeenth-century Church of Grace, restored during the nineteenth century. This church has some fine eighteenth-century altar pieces, and old paintings can be found in the vestry. Vincente Galez was the

60

inspiration for many artists, and the altar in the Church of Grace is made in the Galez style.

One of Tegucigalpa's first cemeteries is situated beside the Church of Calvary on Avenida 2. This church was constructed in 1746 and its stone cross once stood in the Church of St Francis, the oldest of the city's churches. The Church of St Francis was begun as early as 1592 by Franciscan friars, but was rebuilt in 1740. The money to build it was donated by miners who had made their fortune in the gold and silver mines, and its gold altarpieces date from the eighteenth century. There is now a school next door to the church, where once the convent of St Francis stood.

In contrast to the colonial style of the churches, the National Congress is a house on stilts, and has a very modern appearance. It stands on the Avenida Juan Roman Molina. The National University building is beside it. It was designed in the mid-nineteenth century in Spanish style, and painted green. However, the University of Tegucigalpa has spread so rapidly, that a new university (Ciudad Universitaria) has had to be built on the road to Suyapa so that all the students enrolled in the university can be admitted.

Tegucigalpa is lucky to have two other parks besides the Parque Central. The Parque la Concordia is well liked by students who come to read and study, and old people who sit on the benches and chat. Parque la Concordia, although a small park, is notable for its sculptures, which are replicas of Maya and Aztec structures. Some of the sculptures are copies of the altars from the Maya city of Copán, and the Mexican city of Chichen-Itzá, and represent Aztec art.

From the Parque Central it is not far to the Parque la Leona. Most places are easy to reach by foot in Tegucigalpa, through the winding, cobbled streets. La Leona is a residential area, full of elegant colonial houses, many of which have been carefully restored by their owners. From the Parque la Leona there are wonderful views over the city.

Hondurans like bargaining, and the markets of Tegucigalpa are always crowded. In the area known as Comayaguela is the Mercado de Artesanias Populares. It is full of handicrafts from all over Honduras—leather goods, paintings by local artists, woodcarvings, furniture and textiles. Even though the articles have price tags, Hondurans expect people to bargain.

The largest market is the Mercado San Isidro which spreads

This beautiful interior is typical of Honduras' cathedrals

A market in Tegucigalpa

itself over several blocks. People come here from all over Honduras, to buy fresh vegetables, handicrafts, textiles and furniture at low prices. This is the bargain basement of Honduras, and everyone takes advantage of it.

Also in Comayaguela is the National Museum and Anthropological Institute, which was once the home of former president Julio Lozano. It is small, but contains interesting pre-Columbian objects from the Maya city of Copán.

The Monumento a la Paz (Peace Monument) stands on a

A peasant woman bringing her produce to market in Tegucigalpa

hill called Cerro de Juana Lainez, which overlooks the city. But an even better view can be had from the Parque Naciónes Unidas (United Nations Park) which is right on top of Mount Picacho, at an altitude of 1,300 metres (4,300 feet). In this park there are playing fields, examples of Maya art, flower gardens, and picnic areas. On weekends many Hondurans arrive by bus from the city to get some fresh air and indulge in their favourite sport, *futbol*. Afterwards they get together in the picnic areas to enjoy an outdoor meal of *tamales, curiles* (sea-food), *tortillas*, or whatever else they have brought with them.

Comayagua, the former capital, is Tegucigalpa's twin city, and was founded in 1537 by Alonso de Caceres. Much of its colonial character has been retained in its houses and Spanish-style churches. Its cathedral was built by Indian labourers between 1685 and 1715, and decorated with carvings of ears of corn, simple angels and Indian symbols. It is believed that some of the symbols indicate the Immaculate Conception because Comayagua takes as its patron saint the Virgin of the Immaculate Conception, and celebrates her at its Feast Day held on December 8, each year. Comayagua's cathedral has several statues made by the Indians, known as *naifs*, which are carried through the streets of the city during the Good Friday processions. It has many other treasures too. The main altar dates from 1704. Philip II of Spain gave the church a clock— now in the church tower—which was made by the Moors in the twelfth century, for the Palace of the Alhambra in Seville, Spain. Philip IV presented the church with a crucifix.

Every church has a bell, but the oldest bell in the Americas is in the Church of St Francis, built in 1569. On it is inscribed *"fundida 1462 Alcala"*, showing it was made in Spain in the fifteenth century.

The Church of Grace, built between 1550 and 1558, was the first cathedral of Honduras and stands on one side of the town's main square, the Plaza de Armas. Near the cathedral stands the Museum of Colonial and Religious Art which holds a large collection of religious objects, dating from the sixteenth century to the present day.

The Museum of History and Archaeology has a collection of ceramics and stone figurines, as well as tools and jewellery. It is especially interesting as it shows the way Hondurans lived, displaying not only their working implements, but how they dressed and the personal objects they carried with them. The costumes of the men through the ages bring Honduran history to life. The archaeological finds are fascinating too, for they show how cities were unearthed and how ancient objects which had been buried for centuries were discovered.

Comayagua, with its adobe and stucco houses, cobblestone streets and tiny *plazas* (squares) has preserved its past, just as Valle de Angeles (Valley of the Angels), a short distance from Tegucigalpa, has done. Valle de Angeles is now an important handicraft centre. In this seventeenth-century atmosphere there exists a flourishing artisan industry, with a handicraft school where young Hondurans learn cabinet-making, wicker-work, woodcarving and jewellery design.

Santa Lucía, 16 kilometres (10 miles) from Tegucigalpa, is a small colonial village. During the sixteenth century it was an active mining town, but the mines no longer operate. However, they can still be seen and it is not hard to imagine these old mines when they were fully operational during the time of the Spaniards in Honduras.

Santa Lucía is a Highland town standing at 1,370 metres

Woodcarving—a traditional craft in Honduras

(4,500 feet), almost hidden in the mountains. Its old church faces down the valley and its winding cobbled streets are lined with orchids and other exotic flowers. In this mountain setting with its brisk, bracing air, it seems as if the houses are clinging to the mountain sides for support, so steep is the terrain. In its church there are several interesting paintings, one of which is believed to have been donated by Philip II of Spain. The Santa Lucía market, brimming with fresh vegetables, takes place on Sundays and people from all around come and buy.

Closer to Tegucigalpa is Suyapa Church, situated on a hill

67

overlooking the valley. This church possesses the tiny image of the Virgin of Suyapa measuring only a finger length. It was found on a mountain in 1747. Today it stands on the main altar and is believed to possess healing powers. The Virgin of Suyapa is the patron saint of Honduras, and attracts many pilgrims each year from all over the country.

Thirty-two kilometres (twenty miles) from Tegucigalpa is another mining town, Ojojona, where Francisco Morazan lived. Ojojona has several colonial churches, the finest of which is the Church of Calvary.

Comayagua also has its festivals. The Day of Immaculate Conception is its most important celebration. An Indian

A typical village church—painted white and built in colonial style

procession takes place on December 12 and the main fiestas are those celebrating the feast days of San Sebastian, San Blas and the Virgin of Lourdes.

Both Comayagua and the capital have a reserved, yet easy-going air. Tegucigalpa has modern hotels and good communications. The Highlanders are proud of their mountain city, and the way it is slowly, but surely advancing.

To understand how modern-day Honduras developed, let us take a closer look at its most ancient city—the capital of the lost Maya Empire.

Copán—City of the Maya

Copán lies 225 kilometres (140 miles) from Tegucigalpa, and 190 kilometres (120 miles) from San Pedro Sula, and is situated in a valley 640 metres (2,100 feet) above sea level. This area, densely wooded with forests of hardwood and pitchpine, is often hunted for game. The forests are full of animals and birds, and the Copán river has an abundance of fish.

The Maya established Copán as their capital. In the Early Classical Period of A.D. 300 to 500, they made remarkable discoveries in astronomy and mathematics which rivalled those of ancient Egypt. They developed the zero (0) which was not introduced into Europe until the Middle Ages. They perfected a calendar with each day ruled by a particular god. They also began to record information by hieroglyphics (characters used in picture writing). These writings are believed to have been written on parchment. Unfortunately few have survived because they were burned by the Spaniards. Those that did survive were difficult to decipher, for the Maya had developed a highly specialized code.

Their ceramics, paintings and architecture were superb. They were not only astronomers, but also engineers and builders, and their ruined stone buildings testify to their amazing knowledge and advanced skills.

70

The ruins at Copán, capital city of the Maya. This picture shows a stairway with ornamental sculptured markings

During their Classical Period from the sixth to the tenth centuries, the Maya constructed towns and cities. Familiar with engineering, they built clay-lined reservoirs and causeways so water could run freely from the mountains. Their towers, the tallest ever constructed, were the forerunners of the skyscrapers of the modern world. They also knew how to irrigate land. They cultivated vast areas of fertile terrain and grew an abundance of crops.

Maya cities were characterized by stepped pyramids and temples. There was always a main *plaza* which was wide and

71

spacious, and important for the many activities, meetings and ceremonies held there. There were also several smaller squares. In the centre of these, the Maya erected carved altars and stelae (upright stone tablets) which they inscribed. There they worshipped their gods, and buried their dead beneath the pyramids. Their political leaders were given elaborate funerals, and because the Maya possessed many decorative objects such as gold and jewels, their warriors and leaders were buried with their splendid possessions.

The stone cities of the Maya served as administrative centres as well as religious ones. Only the leaders, priests and artisans actually lived in the cities, while the ordinary people lived in small huts outside. Although there were many other important cities, Copán is believed to have been the scientific centre of the Maya world.

With such an advanced way of life, it is a mystery how and why the Maya disappeared. Some believe the common people rose up against their leaders and destroyed them, but no one knows for certain exactly what happened. Nor can anyone tell how the Maya might have further influenced the world's cultural, scientific and astronomic developments had they survived. As it is, all that remains is their ruined cities.

By the time the Spaniards arrived in Honduras, Copán was abandoned, and the once splendid Maya city overgrown by the jungle. Information was sent back to Spain, reporting on what the Spaniards had seen, but nothing was done and Copán was left to rot. In the nineteenth century, explorers from Britain and America set out for the city, and soon excavations were started by a group of archaeologists.

It is clear why the Maya chose Copán as the site for their great capital. The surrounding countryside, with its fertile soil, was ideal for growing maize, their staple food. The forests protected them. The valley was sheltered and formed a river basin which made irrigation easy. Forests provided game, and wood for building. Rivers provided fish. The volcanic rock of the area could easily be cut into building blocks and then carved and sculpted. Furthermore, the rock proved to be perfect for their stone tools to work on, for the Maya had no metal implements for such purposes. Thus they were able to build their immense cities. It is estimated that no fewer than 500,000 people lived in Copán between the sixth and tenth centuries.

The city extended right across the valley and contained temples, palaces, stelae and monuments. Today Copán Archaeological Park in north-west Honduras, close to the Guatemalan border, shows what the Maya world must have been like. It has a ceremonial centre containing temples, stelae, mounds, calendar stones, pyramids and ball courts.

Ball courts were designed for a special game known to the Maya and later to the Aztecs of Mexico. The Ball Court at Copán, now restored, is one of the longest ever found, and dates from A.D. 775. It measures 25 metres (81 feet) long, and 6.5 metres (21 feet) wide. During the games, many spectators would gather to watch the Maya players competing for prizes. The game seems to have been similar to squash. The player bounced

The Ball Court at Copán

the ball up against the wall to hit a marker (a carved figure). He was not allowed to use his hands, and the idea was to keep the ball in play between two teams, each consisting of three to five players. As the ball was large and heavy (made of rubber), and there was bodily contact with it, the game was rough and dangerous. Players wore protective clothing—thick leather gloves and knee pads. Although the game was of religious importance, it is not thought that the Maya, unlike the Aztecs, sacrificed losers to the gods. However, evidence has been found which indicates that other sacrificial offerings were made.

In addition to the Ball Court, Copán is composed of the Great Plaza, the Central Court, the Western Court and the Eastern Court. The main square (Plaza de Ceremonias) is rectangular, and consists of a wide open area, three sides of which have tiered

74

stone seats. It was probably used as an amphitheatre in the time of the Maya. Six stelae, each measuring between 2.5 and 3.5 metres (about 9 to 12 feet) high, stand in the plaza, carved with the figures of Maya leaders. Their arms are folded and on their heads are tall, feathered head-dresses. They are wearing heavy wristbands, and necklaces and pendants on their chests. On the other side of the stelae are Maya hieroglyphics. These denote birds, serpents, gods, warriors and symbols representing the sun and the moon. Most of these upright stones have an area

**A carved stele.
These figures of stone
represent Maya leaders**

beneath them in which food, jewellery and pottery were placed.

South of the main square is the Central Patio, another large *plaza* containing four stelae, all showing hieroglyphics and carvings. One of the most spectacular glyphs (ornamental sculptured markings) is situated in an area 142 metres (465 feet) long, and 35 metres (114 feet) wide. The stairway is more than 9 metres (30 feet) wide, and has sixty-three steps. It rises to a height of 18 metres (60 feet) above the *plaza*, and was constructed from 2,500 blocks of stone, all beautifully carved, with hieroglyphics relating to astronomy. Inscriptions suggest that

The Maya used stone tools to carve beautiful glyphs (ornamental sculptured markings) like these

the stairway was constructed in the Early Classical Period of the Maya, some time between A.D. 500 and 800. At the top of the stairway, eight steps lead to a temple. Below, at every twelfth step, stands a statue of a male figure.

The Western Court is situated 10 metres (33 feet) above the main square. Snails, instead of birds and reptiles, decorate the stairs. There is also an altar which displays carvings of Maya scientists at work, and a temple which is Copán's highest pyramid. The Eastern Court measures 42 metres (138 feet) long, and 33 metres (108 feet) wide. It contains the Jaguar Stairway decorated with carvings of jaguars. Copán also has a citadel, known as the Acropolis, where tombs have been discovered.

Close to the ruins of Copán is the town of San José de Copán, usually known simply as Copán. It was built in the last century and its museum contains objects from the ruined city. These consist mainly of obsidian (a volcanic rock which resembles bottle glass). There are knives used by the Maya, pendants, sculptures, even teeth filled with fragments of jade.

By no means as ancient as Copán, but one of the oldest colonial cities, is Trujillo. Founded in 1524 by Francisco de las Casas, it was once an early capital of Honduras. Christopher Columbus' fleet sailed into the Bay of Trujillo in 1502 and, once Trujillo was established, it became an important port, handling the gold which came from the mines of the Olancho Valley and sending it to Spain. So ferocious were the pirate attacks—like the conquistadors, the pirates wanted to get their hands on the treasures—that Trujillo was obliged to build fortresses to defend

77

itself. The remains of these three forts—La Concepción, San José, and San Hipolito—can still be seen. Looking at them, it is easy to imagine those pirate advances.

Trujillo still maintains some of its colonial atmosphere, but over the years it has become run down. As the Bay of Trujillo is still unspoiled, the beaches around the town are much used, especially at weekends. But in general the area is little populated and, with so few people, its natural splendours are those which catch the eye—the many species of birds in the Guaymoreto lagoon, the mountains, rivers and jungle.

The Mosquito Coast and the Bay Islands

East of Trujillo lies the Mosquito Coast. It is an area in which the Black Caribs, descendants of the West Indians, settled. They live in villages strung out along the coast and rely mainly on fishing for their livelihood.

Until the Spaniards arrived, the Indians controlled the area, which consisted of stretches of unexplored coast, rivers and lagoons. Even today vast areas of land, including Olancho and Gracios a Dios (Thanks to God), are unexplored jungle regions and mountain ranges. Many aeroplanes have crashed in the impenetrable jungles and never been found. For all that, the Mosquito Coast attracts adventurers and explorers who hope

A Black Carib woman looking out of her window

to find deserted cities and traces of the Maya in its steamy jungles and swamps.

Honduras also has waterfalls and lakes. One of the most spectacular waterfalls is at Balfate, where the water cascades from a height of 60 metres (200 feet) into a lagoon. The largest lake is Lake Yojoa which measures 19 kilometres (12 miles) long and 11 kilometres (7 miles) wide. Surrounded by high mountains, 610 metres (2,000 feet) above sea level, the lake is thought to be of volcanic origin. In this area the air is fresh and healthy, unlike in the humid jungles. Its alpine atmosphere makes it the ideal place for recreation. Hondurans go there to swim, water-ski and canoe. They fish in the lake for black bass and carp.

Hondurans are fresh-air people who like to spend time out of doors. They also enjoy impromptu snacks while driving or strolling around the mountain areas. Because Lake Yojoa is so well stocked with fish, enterprising salesmen set up stands on the highway where fried fish delicacies can be bought.

From the lake area it is only a short distance to other natural beauty spots. The Pulhapanzak waterfalls are formed by the Lindo river cascading over cliffs and falling more than 30 metres (100 feet) into a canyon. The area resembles a rain forest with its water and rising mist. Over the years, due to the rushing torrent, natural pools have formed. Many Hondurans prefer to bathe in these rather than in the streamlined hotel swimming-pools.

The wild, natural beauty of the Pulhupanzak Falls area

appealed to the Maya too. Remains have been found close by of a Maya settlement containing a *plaza* and a temple mound. Impressed by the power of natural resources, they were attracted, no doubt, by the thunderous rush of waters over the steep cliffs, as well as by the isolation of the area.

Today the Lake Yojoa area can boast a resort development, Brisas del Lago (Lake Breezes), and two hotels with restaurants serving many varieties of fish, freshly caught from the lake.

Some distance from Lake Yojoa stands the Fortress of San Fernando de Omoa. The king of Spain gave the order for this fort to be built during the years 1759-1777 so that the ports of the Caribbean coast could withstand pirate attacks. From their

The Fortress of San Fernando de Omoa— built to protect the Spanish conquistadors from pirate attacks

hideouts on the Mosquito Coast and the Bay Islands, the pirates terrorized the Caribbean, and the king wanted to put an end to their looting.

In order to build the imposing fort, stones had to be brought from the Spanish Fortress of San Tomas de Castilla in Guatemala 160 kilometres (100 miles) away. To reach Omoa, they could either be transported down the Dulce river or through the hot and steamy jungles. Many thousands of workers were hired to help with the building. Most of them were Blacks, the rest Jicaque Indians. Many died of yellow fever and malaria, for the jungles were very unhealthy places in which to work.

Somehow, despite the setbacks, the fort was completed. It was attacked several times but stood firm until 1779 when, after a battle lasting four days, it fell into the hands of the British. It survived not only attacks but hurricanes, and today its solid walls still stand.

Like the Mosquito Coast, the Bay Islands have hardly altered since Columbus landed on Guanaja in 1502. In 1859, the Islands became self-governing after nine years under British colonial rule. Today many people speak English, and trace their ancestry back to the early English settlers.

These days the inhabitants of the islands are less numerous than they were at the time of Columbus' discovery when Paya Indians lived there. They used their canoes not only for fishing but also as a means of transportation, and it is thought they traded with the Maya. With their large population, the islands prospered. Clay figures, jade and knives have been discovered.

A view of one of the Bay Islands

So too have residential areas, burial grounds and primitive musical instruments, such as conch shells and whistles.

Today, as on most Caribbean islands where there is little to do, the islanders are carefree and friendly. They work as fishermen, and boatbuilders and in the coconut trade.

The islands consist of pine-clad mountains, lush tropical vegetation, clear streams, fertile plains and white, sandy beaches shaded by palm trees. Their coral reefs make them ideal for scuba divers and snorkellers. Unlike the interior of Honduras, the islands are never scorchingly hot as they are cooled by the trade winds, and usually maintain a steady, year-round temperature of 26° Centigrade (78° Fahrenheit).

83

Hundreds of birds live on the Bay Islands, as well as small lizards and rabbits. There are few mosquitoes, but sandflies are a menace on the beaches. As they cannot be seen—the locals call them *no-see'ums*— they can cause untold damage as people do not know they are being bitten. To outsmart these invisible insects, the islanders build their homes on stilts, away from the sand.

The Bay Islands have several deep-water bays. Shipwrecks litter the ocean floor. Roatan, the largest island, has a deep-water harbour in the south of the island called French Harbour. It also has an airstrip. However, the island has only a single paved road which runs from West End to Oak Ridge and on to Punta Gorda. Oak Ridge is built on an estuary, so everyone goes everywhere by boat, some even travelling by dugout canoe. Shrimp boats get ready to sail in the bay, for shrimp is an important catch not only for the Bay Islands but also for Honduras' export markets.

Punta Gorda is a Black Carib community but, unlike other Garifuna villages, Punta Gorda's houses are not built on stilts, but at ground level. Black Caribs do not like isolated living. They prefer to congregate in a village where they can be sure of people around them. At the same time they like being close to the sea. The only inland villages are those of Juticalpa and Corazal. The Black Caribs enjoy a lively atmosphere and do

A road on the Island of Roatan

Shrimp boats anchored in French Harbour. Shrimps are an important export for Honduras

not care to live in the town of West End which, although it has some fine beaches, is a quiet, tranquil place.

The Bay Islanders live life at an unhurried pace. They do not bother with timetables, believing that everything gets done in its own good time. There are no telephones, no television and no newspapers. Letters can take up to two weeks to arrive. Luckily there are telegrams so that visitors can make hotel reservations.

The easternmost island of the archipelago is Guanaja. Its houses are all built on stilts, sometimes over floating waterways. Houseboats are moored on the canals. Boats are a necessity as Guanaja has no roads. It is a beautiful island with sandy beaches, coral reefs, waterfalls and mountains. This island is inhabited

86

by fair-skinned, light-haired descendants of the British and French, as well as by *mestizos*, who comprise by far the biggest proportion of the two thousand strong population.

In contrast to Guanaja which is virtually built on water, the Island of Utila is composed of flat, swampy land. East Harbour is the island's main town, a quiet, peaceful place where nothing much happens. Utila has good beaches, though no coral reefs. The west of the island is largely uninhabited, most people living in the settlements of Pigeon Cay and Suc-Suc Cay, which are connected by a long walkway just like the system on the neighbouring island of Guanaja.

The Bay Islands are volcanic in origin and some of the hills reach 360 metres (1,200 feet). The beaches all have fine, powdery sand, and the clear sea is the colour of deep turquoise.

The settlement of Pigeon Cay on the Island of Utila

The warm waters off the islands are home to many varieties of brilliantly coloured fish, but beware, they also contain sharks!

The main islands of Roatan, Utila and Guanaja can be reached by air from Tegucigalpa, San Pedro Sula and La Ceiba. Boats leave from Puerto Cortés and La Ceiba. Like the mainland, the Bay Islands can expect to see more visitors in the coming years. Honduras is keen to make good use of its natural resources, and both the mainland and the islands have plenty of those.

Moving Towards the Future

For many years, Honduras was known as just another banana republic. During the years of military rule, people began to think of it as a dictatorship where violence was the order of the day, and inhabitants were not free to express their wishes. However, since the changeover of power in 1981, the country has remained politically stable, and the newly elected civilian government has begun to look more fully at the needs of the people.

Today Honduras is gradually beginning to emerge from its banana republic image. A new middle class is developing, with money to invest in the economy. Honduras is looking to expand its industries, and to find new sources of income. A profitable one could be the fast-developing tourist industry, for with its mountains, Caribbean islands and 800 kilometres (500 miles) of beaches, Honduras can take advantage of its natural beauty. The Ministry of Culture and Tourism is keenly interested in improving Honduras' image abroad, and encouraging more foreigners to visit the republic.

In the past, Honduras has sought foreign aid from Britain and the United States in order to supply its basic needs for water supplies and technical equipment. Today the republic is looking to international development agencies for financial help. More accommodation is certainly needed if tourism is to become an important industry, while better transportation in so far undeveloped areas would mean Honduras could begin to make use of its many untapped resources.

However, while expanding, Honduras is trying to keep its individuality, for this is a country with an ancient history and a fascinating past. While there has been rapid growth in San Pedro Sula, the Mosquito Coast has remained undeveloped. Over the next decade, the Honduran government is planning to look closely at the republic's needs, its resources and its industrial growth, so that eventually it will rely less and less on foreign aid and move towards total independence.

Index

92